DIGITAL PHOTOGRAPHY

A Beginner's Guide to DSLR Photography

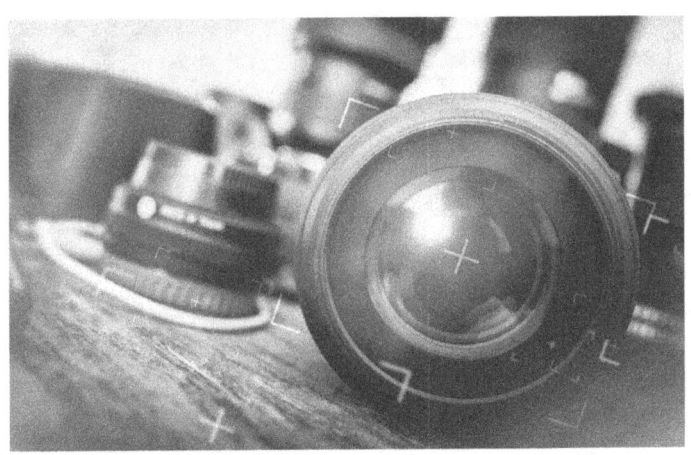

Celeste Jarabese

Table of Contents

Introduction

Did you know that cameras can be complicated? When I first got my DSLR camera, I was frustrated by its many buttons and dials. I could not master what each button and dial does. Even worse, I could not seem to capture what I saw through the viewfinder. Day after day, I kept doing trial and error with nothing coming close to perfection at all! I was tempted to take it back to have it returned. I gave myself a last chance to try and figure things out and making it fun while at it. I did manage to work it out and started taking my very first spectacular pictures.

You may be going through the same, or maybe you are considering getting yourself a DSLR camera and feel scared about the next step! You don't have to be because I have put together this simple guide to help you maneuver your DSLR seamlessly. The truth is, as a beginner in photography, there is a tendency to be a visual learner. My role here is to try as much as possible to make photography easy for you through this guide.

Indeed, when you are considering to begin being a serious photographer, the first and most important thing is to get a good-quality camera. To many people, a DSLR camera is a must-have. However, you have to bear in mind that even though you may know what it does, there are still a lot of things that you should know about the machine.

CHAPTER 1

What is a DSLR Camera?

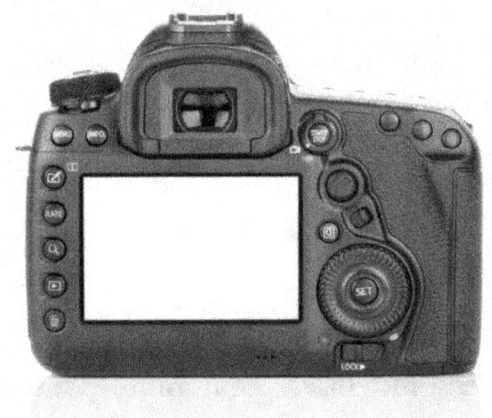

DSLR simply stands for **Digital Single-Lens Reflex**. It is the camera that many photography pros and amateurs dream of using. The good thing with this camera is that you can change the lenses to mimic a wide range of effects and take charge of its aperture and shutter speed.

The first small-format entered the market in 1920 with a 35 mm single-lens reflex. It was not until 1999 that Nikon released the very first DSLR camera. At the time, the camera cost

$6000 with an effective 2.74 megapixels. What is interesting is that the digital versions still maintained the mirror system. They utilized a single lens for both frame and capture of the subject. Today, things have evolved, and we have Canon EOS 5DS R camera joining this club. It costs about $4000 with a mind-blowing resolution of 50.6 megapixels!

It is important to note that there is a difference between a mirrorless camera and one that has mirrors. The mirrors inside the camera play a significant role in reflecting the light that comes through the lens to the prism and into the viewfinder. This way, the camera allows you to preview your shot. Therefore, when you press the shutter button, the mirror will flip up, causing the shutter to open so that the light can fall onto the image sensor, hence capturing your final image. An example of such a camera is the old Nikon D3400 DSLR and similar new ones today.

On the other hand, a mirrorless camera works by merely allowing the light to pass through the lens and onto the image sensor. This, in turn, captures a preview of the image and displays it on the rear screen. A second screen is found inside the viewfinder; an example of this camera is the Sony Alpha a6300.

The Benefits of a DSLR Camera

There are so many benefits that one gets to enjoy when using a DSLR camera. These benefits are drawn from the fact that the DSLR camera has a bigger sensor that makes it less susceptible to noise than a small compact camera. This is mainly because larger sensors have been found to collect more light, which also means that they respond to low light conditions. Your average iPhone or any other smartphone can also take good pictures. But, in as much as they are ideal for taking a quick snap, they are not your go-to devices when it comes to a more advanced typed of photography.

So, what benefits can we get from having a DSLR camera?

Instant review of work

One of the primary reasons why professional photographers prefer using a DSLR camera to any other is the fact that they have an instant review feature. This advantage makes it possible for one to have maximum use of the right setup, location, and proper light to produce an impeccable number of keepers.

Let's rewind a little. Do you recall the days of film photography? During those times, the photographer had to exercise lots of caution before making an exposure. He/she had to ensure that the exposure was dead-on accurate and had to get the focus precisely! Once the correct exposure has been achieved, there was no way to get back to it to redo the shoots if things did not turn out the way you wanted them to be.

When using a traditional camera, the photographer is forced to take as many shots as possible to be on the safe side of things. However, with the DSLR camera, you get to enjoy the instant review features that allow you to check your shoot results at the back of the camera. Moreover, with the advent of wireless connections, you can tether your shoot so that you can check your work on a computer.

The ability to shoot in RAW and post process later

One thing that also set the DSLR camera apart from all other cameras is that it can shoot in RAW. This way, it allows a lot of opportunities for editing the pictures. With film photography, one is limited to just a few basic darkroom editing options.

The DSLR's RAW file is an image format that allows all the data collected by the sensor to be retained in its unprocessed and uncompressed form.

The JPEG format does not allow you to make significant changes and corrections to the images that you have taken. This is mainly because the format itself is compressed, which means that there are lots of data generated as a result.

On the other hand, if you take RAW and JPEG photos, you will notice that the RAW images have a softer tag. They also have subdued colors, which means that you can use your post-processing workflow to enhance it, including using Photoshop tricks, which JPEG will never allow you to do.

The other advantage of the post-processing feature is that it offers you the ability to even out the exposure while ensuring that you recover details from shadows. With a RAW image, you get between 12-14 bits of information compared to about 8 bits of JPEG information. This means that you have a chance to play around with a wide range of luminance, which allows you to avoid things like posterization, hence gaining control over the histogram.

The other benefit of shooting in RAW is that it allows you to play around with the white balance. You may be thinking, "But, what is a white balance?" Well, white balance is one of the most challenging aspects of photography that most professionals find hard to manage. Most professionals prefer shooting with a gray card and 18% to adjust the white balance during the post-processing stage. To leverage this, you have to have a DSLR camera.

Fast auto-focusing mechanism

The third benefit of using a DSLR camera is that it primarily uses Phase detection sensors for auto-focusing. The phase-detection plays a significant role in permitting you to lock on focus so fast using the detection sensors located at the base of the camera. In other words, as light travels through the lens, it bounces off the mirror. Some of that light goes through and is reflected off in another mirror located at the camera's base. It then reaches several dedicated phase-detection sensors that boost focusing.

You do not have this advantage when using a point and shoot system because what it has is contrast-detection, which is a slower system. Today, mirrorless systems are closing this gap with the help of an on-sensor dual-pixel phase-detection system.

Impeccable collection of lenses

The only difference between a DSLR and an SLR camera is the presence of a digital sensor and an LCD screen on the DSLR camera. In other words, most of the companies that make cameras have chosen to retain the lens mounts on the digital cameras. This way, it ensures that the lenses used in either case remained usable even on newer camera models.

Nowadays, DSLR cameras have a more extensive type of lenses. Therefore, ensuring that people can choose a type of lens suited for the kind of photography they are into.

CHAPTER 2

Steps on How to Use Your DSLR Camera

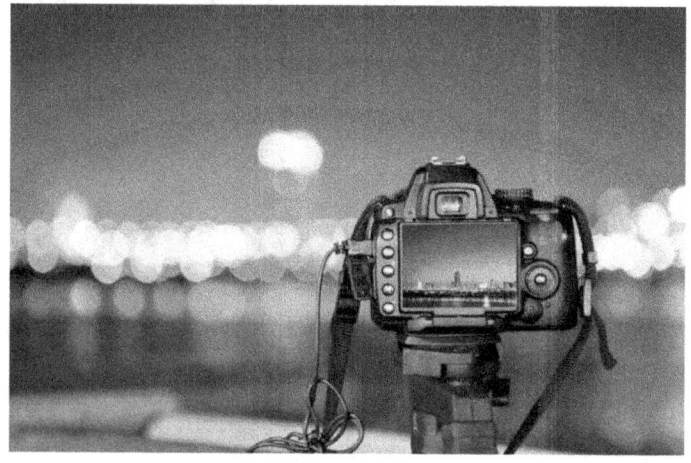

If you are considering buying a DSLR or have already bought one, you have to notice that you have to learn lots of things. Some of these include the following:

- Shooting Modes
- Understanding ISO
- Exposure Triangle
- Metering and Exposure Compensation
- File Size and Type

- White Balance

Step 1: Learn the Shooting Modes

When it comes to using a DSLR camera, you should start by learning the shooting modes. The shooting modes are likely to be found on top of the camera with a dial labeled "Auto, Tv, M, Av, and P, among others. By selecting the shooting mode, it determines how your camera settings will respond upon pressing the shutter. For instance, when you choose "Auto," your camera will automatically set the exposure and the shutter and aperture speed.

You may be thinking, "my DSLR has a different dial mode compared to other DSLRs." Well, that is true, and it should not be something to get worried about. This is mainly because different manufacturers have different labeling systems. Like, instead of Av, P, M, and Tv, you might get something like A, P, M, and T/S. The good thing is that they all function in the same way. For this, it would greatly help to check your manufacturer's product guide or manual.

So, what do these modes mean?

Aperture priority (A or Av)

This mode is often thought about as the semi-automatic shooting mode. When you select this mode, you simply have set the aperture, and the camera will automatically select its shutter speed. Therefore, aperture refers to the lens opening's size through which light passes whenever the shutter is opened. In other words, if the aperture is larger, then more light passes through.

The aperture is often measured in f-stops and hence displayed using an f-number, which translates to the ratio of focal length and the aperture/opening diameter. This means that the larger the aperture, the smaller the f-number. On the other hand, the smaller the aperture, the larger the f-number. When you reduce the aperture by one f-stop, the amount of light passing into the camera is halved.

Therefore, when it comes to photography, the aperture is one of the major components that affect the "depth of field." In other words, the aperture has a direct effect on the amount of image in focus. When the depth of field is large, then there is a considerable distance within the scene in focus. On the contrary, if the depth of field is shallow, it will show an image with a sharp focus and a soft background that is out of focus. In most cases, this is used when shooting portraiture or wildlife so that you can precisely isolate your subject from the background. Moreover, when you use the aperture priority, you gain control over the depth of field, and the camera takes care of the rest.

Shutter Priority (Tv or S)

Just like the aperture priority, the shutter priority is another semi-automatic shooting mode. In this case, the photographer sets the shutter speed while the camera takes care of the aperture. The shutter speed is measured in seconds and refers to the amount of time the shutter is open when taking a snap. This means that more light passes through the aperture to the sensor if the shutter stays open for longer.

If you intend to freeze a fast-moving object, you should select a shorter shutter speed. For instance, when shooting a racing car, moving wildlife, or actions. It would be best to have your camera on a tripod to hold steady when the shutter is open. However, if you want to blur an object on the move, such as a waterfall, you should use a longer shutter speed. Therefore, in a Tv or S mode, you set the shutter speed while the camera determines the right aperture for the correct exposure.

Program (P)

This mode is almost halfway between full manual control and semi-automatic modes. In this mode, you can set the aperture or shutter speed so that the camera can maintain the right exposure by simply making adjustments to the other one accordingly. So, if you change the aperture, the shutter speed will change automatically, and vice versa. Therefore, you gain additional freedom that using either the shutter or the aperture priority does not offer without necessarily switching between the two shooting modes.

Manual (M)

Just as the name suggests, the manual mode gives you full control over determining the exposure and setting both the shutter speed and the aperture priority. In this case, there is an exposure indicator within the viewfinder or on the screen, which tells you whether the image is under-or over-exposed. However, you have the freedom to change the shutter speed and the aperture for you to achieve the correct exposure.

Tip: *The first step to learning how to use your camera is to take it off auto mode. This is because the aperture and the shutter priority offer you two ways of understanding how the different settings on your DSLR affect your images.*

Step 2: Understand the ISO

The ISO refers to the measure of the sensitivity of your camera's sensor to light. This term was derived from film photography, where films with varying sensitivities were used based on the shooting conditions, which is not different in digital photography. ISO is represented numerically from ISO 100 to represent low sensitivity up to ISO 6400 and above representing high sensitivity. It controls the amount of light needed by the camera's sensor to achieve the correct exposure.

16

When the sensitivity is low, it means that more light is needed to achieve the right exposure. On the other hand, high sensitivity means that a lesser amount of light is required to get the desired exposure. To understand this better, let's discuss the difference between low ISO and high ISO numbers.

High ISO numbers

It is commonly used when shooting under low light conditions, such as in a dark room where there is not much light available. When the ISO number is high, like ISO 3200, the sensor's sensitivity is increased. This way, the camera allows a small amount of light to multiply to get a correctly exposed image.

However, using a very high ISO could affect the quality of the images because of increased noise. This could lead to an image that looks grainy. This effect is even more pronounced as the room gets darker with several shadow regions.

Low ISO numbers

It is commonly used when you are shooting outdoors, where there is plenty of light available to hit the sensor during exposure. This would also mean that the sensor does not have to be so sensitive for you to get the right exposure. It is recommended that you use ISO 100 or ISO 200 to get a high-quality image with minimal noise during the daytime.

Tip: You must keep the ISO number as low as possible. This is because the lower the ISO, the lesser the noise, giving a high-quality image as a result. When out on a sunny day, start with a lower ISO number, and see how that goes. If the day is cloudy, begin with an ISO of around 400-800. As you move indoors, consider increasing the ISO number to about 1600 and above.

The good thing is that most of the DSLR cameras today have an "Auto-ISO" function, which allows you to set the camera's ISO based on the amount of available light you are shooting in so you can keep it at the lowest possible. It is important to note that Auto-ISO is important when starting with your camera because it allows you to define your upper limit.

Step 3: Learn the Exposure Triangle

The exposure triangle includes the aperture, ISO, and shutter speed. They all work together to control the amount of light passing through into the camera to get the right exposure.

These parts are linked together, which means that you must understand the interrelationship between them to control your DSLR better. One thing to remember is that you alter the other two when you change one of the settings. For instance, if you reduced the depth of field and chose to use an aperture of f/5.0, this would mean that the aperture size increases, causing an increase in the amount of light getting into the camera. Therefore, for the exposure to be balanced, you could either reduce the shutter speed by a certain factor or lower the ISO by a similar factor.

In other words, all these have the net effect of lowering the amount of light getting into the camera and hence countering the aperture change. It is only a matter of understanding how these three factors are interlinked and that changing one causes a difference in the other two.

Additionally, you must understand that you do not have to adjust the exposure first when using a combination of semi-automatic modes and ISO. However, once you have understood the relationship between aperture and ISO and the shutter speed, you are a step closer to mastering how to use your DSLR.

Step 4: Master the Metering

To reiterate what we have discussed above, your DSLR can calculate the exposure based on the amount of light. However, the question that you must be asking is what exactly it is doing.

When taking a photo, the camera tries as much as possible to calculate the average exposure using some automatic exposure calculation. In other words, it tries to assess both the dark and the light areas to determine the exposure. This process is important to ensure the whole image's tones averages 18% grey, referred to as the middle grey.

This step is what is called metering. Metering is the reason why when you point the camera at a bright white background to take a photo, the image resulting from this will always appear darker than it looks. In the same way, when you point a camera towards a very dark scene to take a photo, the image resulting from it will be brighter than it looks.

The main reason for this is that the camera is averaging the scene, and often, this results in an image that appears as though it is correctly exposed. However, you have to bear in mind that you can control the scenes that are assessed by the camera so that it influences the way the exposure is metered.

There are three types of metering modes. These include the following:

Spot Metering

This refers to a situation where the camera can use a very small area of the scene, in most cases a circle in the middle of the viewfinder that makes up about 5% of the viewfinder area. In other words, it assesses the dark and the light tones in the area and then exposes the whole scene to about 18% grey, starting from the assessment.

Average

In this case, the camera will assess the whole image's tones from one corner to the other and then expose the scene to about 18% grey from that assessment.

Center-Weighted

In this mode, the camera will weigh the exposure reading until the area in the middle of the viewfinder totals to about 80% of the scene. However, the corner of the image is ignored in this case.

Tip: *When you start with your DSLR camera, you must remember the average, and the center-weighted metering modes are the best starting points. This is mainly because they offer a relatively consistent measure of exposure that is needed when you select one mode and stick with it. This way, you get to understand that when a scene is underexposed* *or overexposed, it is different from the way you see it with your naked eye.*

The most important question is, "What do I do if the area is underexposed or overexposed?"

Well, this is where exposure compensation comes into play. This is generally located on a small + or − button that is next to the shutter. It is one of the most important functions when it comes to learning how to use your DSLR. It permits you to either increase or decreases the default meter reading on your camera so that it can account for the actual brightness of the scene.

In other words, if a scene is made up of bright tones yet it is being rendered dark, you can simply apply positive exposure compensation to it so that the camera knows that the scene is required to be lighter than the middle grey.

On the other hand, if the scene that needs to be captured is primarily dark and is being rendered light, you can simply apply negative exposure compensation to allow the camera to recognize that the scene needs to be darker than the middle grey.

Step 5: Learn How to Focus

It does not really matter what shooting mode or the ISO you use because the chances are that there will be a specific subject you are interested in focusing on. This means that if that focus is not achieved, the image will not be anything close to what you want.

Some of the focus modes that you need to understand include:

Autofocus modes

It is important to note that DSLRs come in quite a wide range of autofocus modes. However, for the sake of simplicity, the two that are very key are AF-C and AF-S.

AF-C

AF-C stands for **autofocus-continuous**. This function is best when you take photos of things or objects in motion/action like wildlife and sports. Therefore, when you press the shutter halfway, the focus is acquired and locked on a particular subject such that when the subject moves, the focus adjusts with it. In other words, it will keep refocusing until the photo is taken.

AF-S

It merely stands for **autofocus-single**. It is best to take photos of stationary objects like people, buildings, landscapes, and others. Therefore, when you press the shutter halfway, the focus is acquired and locked at that point for as long as the button is held down. However, if you want to change the focus, you simply release the button, recompose and press the button halfway.

Caution: *You must know the difference between these and **AF/MF** switches found on the lens. **AF** simply stands for autofocus, while **MF** stands for manual focus. The switch overrides when you want a manual focus on your lens.*

Focus points

The above-discussed focus modes rely on the focus points. Therefore, when you look through a viewfinder, you must see the number of dots and squares that are overlaid across the scene. This means that when you press the shutter halfway, you should be able to see one of the squares highlighted in red. This represents the current focus point, and this is where the camera is focusing on within the frame.

You will notice that a new DSLR comes with over 50 focus points. Because of this number, so many people are tempted to leave the focus on automatic focus point selection. However, you must understand that you are the only one that knows what you are trying to focus on. Here, the best option is to ensure that you focus on the right subject rather than using a single focus point.

When you select a single focus point, you should be able to easily change the active point by using one of the directional buttons. Alternatively, if you choose a focus point on your intended subject, it ensures that the camera focuses where you want it to. After several rounds of practice, it becomes easier for you to change the focus point without necessarily taking the camera off your eye.

Tip: *At first, you must set your camera to a single focus point. This is because it will allow you to choose what you are focusing on hence ensuring that the desired subject to be captured is in focus. Once you familiarize yourself with the various focusing modes available and the focus point selection, it becomes easy to explore more advanced modes than the camera can offer.*

Step 6: Understand different file sizes and types

A DSLR camera offers you the option to change the size of the image it records and the file type. Therefore, it is recommended that you set the camera to the largest possible file size. This is because it ensures that you make the most of the megapixels you have at your disposal.

Additionally, you have the option of selecting the setting to record the images as RAW or in jpeg. In other words, it will either record the files as uncompressed so that it contains a lot of image data, which permits for more flexibility during post-processing, or take it in the form of jpeg, which is a compressed file format that is processed automatically by the camera. The good thing is that there will also be a print-ready image straight out of the camera. These are usually much smaller than files, which means that you can fit as many images as you can per memory card.

Tip: *When you are just starting with your DSLR, jpeg is often straight forward. This allows you to get the best results as you keep climbing up the learning curve with your camera before having matters complicated during the post-processing of raw files.*

Step 7: Learn what White Balance does

If you are shooting in jpeg, you must set the white balance before taking the photo. This way, the white balance will correct the color tone of your pictures. Maybe, you have noticed some bluish tone on your images before, and in others, everything appears orange in color. This has to do with a factor referred to as the white balance. While you can make a few adjustments to your computer's image, it is simple if you get things right from the beginning.

The other thing is based on the fact that there are different sources of light ranging from sunlight to bulb light and fluorescent strips, among others. These light sources emit light at different wavelengths hence resulting in a wide range of color temperatures. For instance, the light emitted by the sun or a candle is very warm and has a red or orange wavelength. This kind of colored light is reflected off a surface, and the brain can recognize it automatically to counter the effect. This simply means that you can see the white surface as it is a white surface.

However, the DSLR camera will not function unless it is told otherwise. This means that when a red, blue, or orange color tone, among others, is reflected off the surface and cast to the image, you see it as it is because the camera does not know how to correct it to the actual color.

Another important factor to note is that as the color temperatures are many, several presets are built into your camera to help overcome this effect. The main aim is to ensure that the actual colors of the scene being captured are accurately taken. The auto feature like the AWB will try as much as possible to predict the color of light by merely detecting the scene's predominant color and then countering it. The truth is, in some instances, the camera may not be able to make the correct decision, and hence the images you capture are left with inaccurate colors. Therefore, you should set the color balance on your DSLR before taking any photos just to be on the safe side. This includes the following:

Daylight setting to be used for a clear sunny day. This is mainly because bright sunlight on a clear day is closer to the neutral light we get.

The cloudy setting is to be used when shooting on a cloudy day. This ensures that it adds a warm tome to daylight images.

Shade settings are recommended for use when shooting in the shade. This is because shaded areas appear cooler generally or bluer and need a little touch of warmth.

Tungsten settings are to be used when you are shooting indoors, such as under incandescent light bulbs or street lights. This ensures that it cools the yellow tones.

Fluorescent settings are essential for compensating for the green, and blue color tones often derived from the fluorescent light strips, especially when taking photos indoors.

Flash settings are important when you intend to add a cool blue cast to your images and add a touch of warmth.

Tips: *To avoid the auto white balance, you should set it manually. This is because you can tell what the day looks like by just looking at the sky to determine what color balance you need.*

However, if you move indoors, you must consider the lighting you are shooting under to select the right white balance for the situation. This will soon be your second nature to set once you take the camera out of the bag.

Step 8: Learn how to read the Histogram

Even though you take a glance at the camera's LCD screen to check if the image is correctly exposed, you have to understand that this is not a reliable way to assess exposure. This is because the image may appear to be darker or brighter on the screen than it is. Therefore, one of the best ways to accurately tell if the exposure is correct during shooting is by using the histogram on your camera (a graph that shoes next to your image on your camera screen).

When you learn how to interpret the histogram, you will be able to draw information about the image's tonal range. Yes, this is not easy, but you will soon master how to interpret the histogram and use it to take professional photos with a little bit of practice. You have to bear in mind that the left side of the graph represents the shadows while the right side is the highlights.

It is important to note that if the graph is skewed to the right, the image under capture may be overexposed. This means that you will have lost so many details in the image's lighter region. On the other hand, if the image is skewed to the left, the chances are that the image is underexposed and hence the photo resulting will be too dark.

Step 9: Play around with perspective

One of the best ways to get a little bit more creative when it comes to photography is to try different perspectives. Trust me, you can be on the same scene, but when you look at things/images from different angles, you can get the best photos out of it. You can choose to approach your subject from above or below and end up changing the entire feel of the photograph.

You have to understand that not every angle will work the same way for every photo. However, the truth is that you will never know what works if you are not willing to try things by experimenting as much as possible. For instance, if you are shooting wildlife, you could try going down to their level so that you can view the world through their own eyes. On the other hand, if you are shooting a portrait, you could choose to stand on a bench to take your shoot from above.

Step 10: Understand what the Rule of Thirds require

The rule of the third states that when a photo is not centered, it is considered to be more interesting and balanced. Now, let us imagine the image that you intend to capture. The image has a grid over it with two horizontal and vertical lines that divide it into eight equal parts. This means that, following the rule of the thirds, instead of positioning the subject at the center of the image, you could choose to place them at one intersection of the four lines. Some DSLRs have grid options that you can turn on and use in composing your image.

Well, photography is indeed about creativity and self-expression. Therefore, you have the freedom to break this rule from time to time so that you can place the points of interest at different points on the photo. While this is okay, it is important that you fully understand it and consciously think about your desired points and the place you would like them to be before you go ahead in breaking this rule.

Step 11: Always place your eyes in focus

When you are shooting portraits, you will essentially be focusing on a small region. This means that getting a sharper image should be your primary interest. The eyes are the most important facial feature and are the very first thing people look at. This is especially the case when people come in close-ups.

Keep in mind that your main focus should be your subject's eyes. Therefore, for you to get a sharp image of the eyes, you must select a single focus point and aim it at one of the eyes. Once you have the right focus on one of the eyes, you can now keep the shutter button half-pressed. Then move your DSLR camera closer so that you can recompose the photo to include the other eye.

Step 12: Pay closer attention to the background

From a general point of view, the background of your image has to be as simple. It should also be free of clutter as much as possible. This ensures that it does not pull the attention of the viewer away from the primary subject. You must choose to use muted colors and plain patterns when taking your shoot mainly because your main aim is to ensure that your viewers pay attention to your model and not the colorful building behind it.

This means that you have to fix the distracting background, something as simple as moving the subject or changing its angle. However, if this does not seem to work well, you can choose to obscure it by merely employing a wider aperture and moving as close to your subject as possible. Try as much as you can to keep the background neutral, especially if you intend to place the subject on the side of the photo so that the background is evident.

Step 13: Use a tripod where you can

For you to get a sharper image when the light is low without necessarily having to increase the ISO as much, a tripod is a must-have accessory. This is mainly because when you use a tripod, you have room to experiment with long exposure. In other words, you can choose to leave the shutter open for seconds to minutes at a time, something that adds some amazing effects to your image, such as landscapes, waterfalls, lakes, and rivers, among others.

Therefore, when you purchase your tripod, you must consider several factors. These factors include; its height, weight, and stability. When it comes to weight, the most critical thing to bear in mind is how you intend to carry it around because whether you like it or not, no one enjoys carrying something heavy. On the other hand, the tripod must be stable enough to support your camera and the lenses you plan to use. If you do not know what tripod to go for, you can check out their product reviews to feel the experiences people have using them.

Step 14: Take a shot at the sunrise and sunset

Did you know that lighting is everything when it comes to photography? Well, you must understand that lighting can make or break your photography. This is why early mornings and late evenings are thought to be the very best times of the day for taking photographs. The hour just before the sun sets and that after sunrise is referred to as the "golden hour." This is mainly because the light is softer and warmer since the sun is lower in the sky.

Therefore, irrespective of whether you are shooting portraits or landscapes, taking your shots in the early mornings or evening can offer your photos a more serene feel with the warm glow and the long shadows cast. This makes your photography easier, but it is not the only time to take photos outdoors.

Step 15: Invest in high-quality photo-editing software

Once you have mastered how to shoot in RAW, post-processing becomes a must. This means that it is essential that you invest in good photo-editing software. One that will allow you to perform some basic edits like adjusting exposure, contrast, white balance, cropping, and getting rid of blemishes.

Most professionals often use such photo-editing software as Adobe Photoshop and Lightroom, among others. However, if your budget is a bit tight, you can try using Photoshop Elements, Paint Shop Pro, or Picasa.

Step 16: Be very selective

You have to bear in mind that every photographer gets some bad shots irrespective of how talented or experienced they are. The main reason why their portfolios are impressive is that they only share their best pieces. They do not share some of the crappy pictures they took of one scene when they were trying to get the best shot.

So, if you want your pieces to stand out when you share them on social media platforms like Facebook and Instagram, you must try as much as possible to narrow them down to just a few impeccable shots. You may have taken hundreds of shots of the same scene, but you do not have to display all of them because this might obscure the great shots you took.

Step 17: Learn from your mistakes

One thing that can be very frustrating when it comes to photography has images that are overexposed, poorly composed, or blurry. However, instead of allowing this to get the best of you, you can use it as a learning tool. No one was born a perfect photographer, not even other fields of expertise. Therefore, the next time you take bad photos, do not be too fast to hit the delete button. Instead, take some time studying the images that you have taken to determine what exactly might have gone wrong so that you can come up with the best way to fix it.

In most cases, there will always be a simple solution lying in wait. The solution could just be taking a different composition or using a faster shutter speed, among others. However, if the problem keeps recurring, you have a better chance of studying different aspects of photography to tweak and strengthen the weaker areas.

CHAPTER 3

Factors to Consider When Selecting the Best DSLR Camera

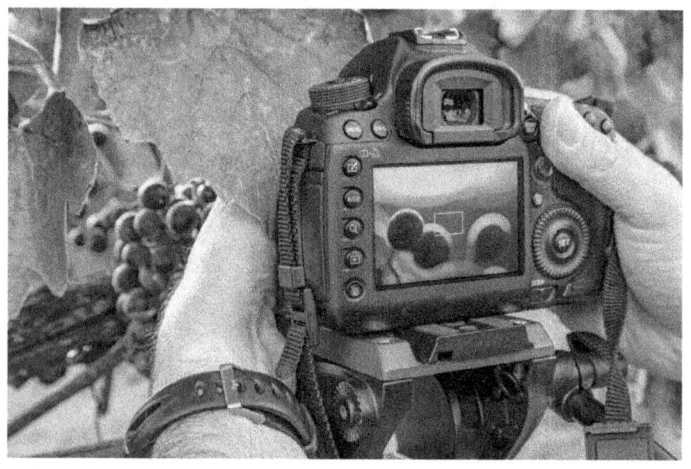

There are so many factors that you have to consider when choosing the best DSLR for your photography. Some of these factors include:

Brand

Many brands are available out in the market ranging from Nikon, Canon to The little guy. So many people get caught up between these brands, not to know which one they should buy.

You are probably torn between purchasing a camera from a big brand or a small brand. That should not be your priority because the most important thing is finding one that has features suitable for your purpose for the camera.

The truth is, soon as you start acquiring lenses and other camera accessories, it becomes quite costly to switch. However, this does not mean that one brand is much superior to the other. The truth is, Nikon makes great DSLRs, but so does Canon, Pentax, and Sony cameras. Yes, one year, it may seem as though one brand is more competitive than the other with every new release, but you will notice that the following year chances are that the ranks will be the other way around.

Yes, brands do matter, but in most cases, not in the way that we like to think. What is important is for you to select a camera based on its features and not necessarily the brand. Before you can make any commitments to purchase, you must try exploring the different lenses and accessories available out in the market.

For instance, if you would like to learn how to take wildlife pictures, the camera you settle for must have a compatible telephoto lens. In this case, you will find that Canon and Nikon are the best options. This is mainly because they are more established, have plenty of lenses, accessories, and flashes to choose from.

Does this mean that you should keep off the smaller brands? Probably not! This is because Pentax, for instance, makes incredible photos with its features such as weather sealing, which are harder to find in popular brands at similar price points.

Sensor Size and Design

When taking a digital photo using a DSLR camera, lights pass through the lens and hit the sensors, which in turn record the image. These camera sensors come in so many different sizes and designs. Well, if you were to compare it to that on your smartphone, the DSLR's sensors are so much larger. These large sensors are better than smaller ones for so many different reasons.

The first image that you capture using a large sensor has a high resolution. This is mainly because if the sensors are large, then the pictures are large, and so is the image quality. Additionally, larger sensors can handle low lighting situations better than any other. When the amount of light coming into the camera is not altered, it simply means that the camera can collect as much light, which is directly proportional to the larger surface area. Additionally, larger sensors have the advantage of giving soft and out-of-focus backgrounds.

The truth is, when it comes to DSLRs, there are two major sensor sizes. The APS-C is the smaller type making them much more suitable for entry-level photographers. This kind of sensor is often found on cameras that are quite easy to operate and are cost-effective.

The other kind is often referred to as the full range sensors about 35mm in diameter and larger. Professional photographers often use them because of a high resolution, which makes them quite expensive. In other words, if your budget is something more than $1600, this could just be the best option for you. However, if you are a beginner, this could just be overkill for you.

You may be thinking, 'if it is overkill, why mention it in the first place?' Well, most camera sensors are either sold as APS-C or a full-frame sensor. Therefore, if you intend to keep growing your skills, you must consider the possibility of updating your lenses later.

While the sensor's size is so important when it comes to photography and selecting the right camera for your purpose, it is critical that you also think about the design of the camera. The backlight sensors are often designed with most of its operational buttons located at the back, making it relatively easy for the light to reach the sensors. The sensors that are backlit perform much better in low lighting conditions than those that are not.

Today, so many camera manufacturers are getting rid of optical low pass filters, and others also go to the extent of eliminating anti-aliasing filters. This filter's main role is to prevent distortion in patterns, something that is otherwise referred to as *moire*. In this case, a common example is a shirt with very fine stripes that appear bent and whirled when a shot is taken.

Sensory technology permits some sort of this distortion to be eliminated so that it can be done without a filter. You have to remember that the filter's main role is to strike a balance between the sensor and light.

Cameras that do not have the optical low pass filter often appear to have more details and richer colors than others. This is why so many manufacturers today are doing away with the filters completely, for instance, the new Nikon's DSLR. This is because the enhanced detail plays a vital role in fashion or product photography, especially in the case of a clothing boutique. This is precisely where the extra moire comes in to play.

Megapixels

So many people wonder whether the megapixels are something to consider when it comes to starting with DSLR. Some aspiring photographers buy cameras based on the megapixels alone, which is a terrible idea for deciding what camera to settle for. It is the megapixels that play a role in determining how much resolution your camera has. The number of pixels multiplied by that on the other side gives you the megapixels count. Cameras with a larger megapixel provide a higher resolution image than those with a lower number. This means that you can print larger photos and crop them without necessarily destroying the image.

That said, you must understand that the megapixels are not as important as the size of the sensor, especially as far as the image quality is concerned. Even a phone with over 40 megapixels isn't going to outcompete a DSLR camera with just 16 megapixels. However, you have to bear in mind that even though the resolution is high, this does not mean that you will produce better images. Apart from all the good things mentioned above, having a DSLR with a high megapixel count increases the chances of noise when the ISO number is high. The good thing is that most cameras today have high megapixels with the capability of reducing noise.

Additionally, when the megapixel count is high, this means that the image file generated is bigger. This may not necessarily be a deal-breaker because all the bigger files produced are flexible during the post-processing phase. The most important thing to remember here is that you will need a bigger memory SD card for high megapixel cameras and a large external drive for storage.

Shooting Speed

The shooting speed defines how fast you can take a snap. Ensuring that you get a camera with a good shooting speed is critical, especially in sports photography and actions. In other words, if you are interested in continuous photography, speed is your priority. This is mainly because speed goes a long way when it comes to capturing action and the best expressions, for that matter.

The speed of a camera is often difficult to measure on paper. The burst speed and the number of photos the camera can take per second serve as good indicators of the camera's overall speed. This is the case when you choose to hold the shutter continuously without releasing it.

Different parts need to be moved each time a DSLR is taking a photo. It is more like a mirror mechanism that so many well-built cameras do not have. There are also big images to consider because it often takes time before a camera can process digital photos like those with a higher megapixel count. Because of these, so many DSLRs have a burst speed of about five fps, which means that it can take approximately five photos in a second.

The more the number of photos a camera can take in a second, the higher your chances of capturing a perfect moment correctly. However, the burst speed may also be an indicator of how fast the camera operates generally.

The measure of how much speed you need is dependent on the kind of photography you intend to practice. If you are into sports, wildlife, and action photography, a DSLR of 10 fps burst speed is an excellent choice. This is mainly because with a faster burst speed, you have a better chance of capturing a perfect moment.

The other speed that you have to look out for is the shutter speed. The shutter speed determines the length of time the shutter stays open to snap a picture. If you have a reasonable budget for a DSLR, then a 1/4000 shutter speed is fast enough to freeze actions and often works well for most kinds of photography. Advanced models even go up to 1/16,000. However, one thing to bear in mind is that the higher the shutter speed, the more the light required. The good thing about them is that they come in handy when shooting outdoors on a very sunny day with a wide aperture enough not to overexpose the image.

Price of a beginner-type DSLR Camera

Many people fail to understand that they are not buying the best camera in the market but getting one that suits their style and budget. There are so many DSLRs available in the market, and their cost is similar to that of a small car. This is because they have lots of advanced features. However, there are those that you can get for just a few hundred dollars, yet they do a pretty good job. They have features that are suitable for a beginner in photography and are very easy to learn.

For instance, for the entry-level/beginner DSLRs, you can get them for as little as $300. Some are quite realistic, and the price range is between $500-1000. As you continue to add features such as the shutter speed, megapixels, and more, the price keeps increasing from there.

If you do not have enough budget for a new DSLR, you can get one that is not current but still has the features you are looking for. It is important to understand that even older DSLR models are still brilliant cameras, and in most cases, you can get an older mid-level DSLR at a very good price. They also have entry-level features that you can easily learn as a beginner.

It is also critical that as you compare the prices, you also consider the features. This is because you expect a new camera to offer you a good boost in image quality as a result of improved technology. A model that is a year older does not have a significant difference from the new ones. However, if the model is two years or older, there is likely a difference in the image quality when not properly set.

Kit Lens and Camera Body

Once you have made up your mind on what DSLR camera to purchase, there is more factor to consider buying the kit or the camera body. In the past, so many beginners go for a DSLR camera and a kit lens. This is mainly because kit lenses are great since they cover the most common zoom range between 18mm and 55mm. They are also cost-effective and are ideal for beginners interested in learning about photography.

However, you have to realize that the kit lens is, in most cases, very limited. This is because their maximum aperture is around f/3.6. You may be wondering what the aperture does and what this means in photography. The truth is that the aperture plays a role in determining how wide the lens opening is. This is because the wider the aperture, the better it is when taking photos in limited light conditions and obtaining a softer out-of-focus background. When you upgrade it further, this makes a huge difference in the image quality. However, the price also increases significantly.

Conclusion

When selecting the best DSLR camera for beginners, you must choose one that matches your style. This way, if you take images like sports, then your main priority should be a camera with a higher shutter speed. On the other hand, if you take photographs of landscapes or still scenes, then what you have to be looking for is the size of the sensor and the megapixel count.

Before selecting a suitable DSLR camera, you must understand factors such as the sensor size, shutter speed, aperture, and ISO, to name a few. However, if you feel nervous about learning photography in the first place, choose a camera that gives you good quality images and has a few buttons and dials on it. This ensures that using the camera is not too overwhelming.

When you understand these features quite well, you will realize that you will choose a camera that will not make your learning process a living hell. Consider reading through the product reviews before you can buy one to feel what experiences people have had with the camera. Remember, you are not buying a camera just because it is the best in the market. Instead, you are getting something that will help you achieve your photography goals.

Make the right choice and enjoy being creative and practice self-expression through photography. Good Luck!